ASTROLOGY AND HEALTH
a beginner's guide

ASTROLOGY
AND HEALTH

 a beginner's guide

DYLAN WARREN-DAVIS

Hodder & Stoughton

A MEMBER OF THE HODDER HEADLINE GROUP

Orders: please contact Bookpoint Ltd, 78 Milton Park, Abingdon, Oxon OX14 4TD.
Telephone: (44) 01235 827720, Fax: (44) 01235 400454. Lines are open from
9.00–6.00, Monday to Saturday, with a 24 hour message answering service.
Email address: orders@bookpoint.co.uk

British Library Cataloguing in Publication Data
A catalogue record for this title is available from The British Library

ISBN 0 340 77484 3

First published 1998
This edition published 2000
Impression number 10 9 8 7 6 5 4 3 2 1
Year   2005 2004 2003 2002 2001 2000 1999

Copyright © 1998 Dylan Warren-Davis

Typeset by Transet Limited, Coventry, England.
Printed in Great Britain for Hodder & Stoughton Educational, a division of Hodder
Headline plc, 338 Euston Road, London NW1 3BH by Cox and Wyman Limited,
Reading, Berks.

To my son Joshua

CONTENTS

Chapter 4   The Air Signs   30

Chapter 5   The Water Signs   34

Chapter 6   The Seven Traditional Planets   38

INTRODUCTION

The subject of health and astrology attracts considerable interest, yet it exists in a sort of cultural vacuum. Today astrology, apparently, has no place within high-tech medicine as most doctors trained within the rigours of scientific thinking would not give the time of day to even think about the subject, let alone apply it. Given this situation it is extraordinary that the subject should exert such an enormous fascination.

This fascination is clearly cultural, as astrology has been linked to health and medicine since the time of the ancient Egyptians. The image of Zodiacal Man below, where the signs of the zodiac are connected to the different parts of the body, can be found in Egyptian hieroglyphs. Zodiacal Man is frequently found in astrological books today which shows the degree to which these astrological ideas still permeate our culture.

Scientific medicine generally has an intense aversion towards astrology, priding itself on how rational thought has triumphed over the superstitions of the past, yet paradoxically it is still using terms that are based upon astrological concepts, for example the term 'flu. Flu is short for *la influenza*, an Italian word referring to the influence of the Moon and Venus in causing phlegmatic, cold and moist diseases in the body. Compared to the few centuries that science has been linked to medicine, astrology has been linked to healing for at least 3,000 years, so it is hardly surprising that astrological ideas are still found within medical terminology.

Despite its decline during the last three centuries, astrology still holds a powerful fascination, as shown by the popularity of 'Sun sign' sections in the media. The symbols contained in astrology are able

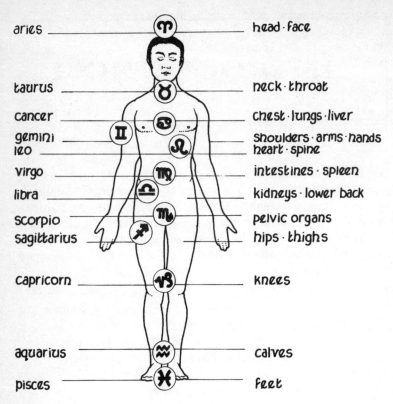

aries — head · face

taurus — neck · throat

cancer — chest · lungs · liver

gemini — shoulders · arms · hands
leo — heart · spine

virgo — intestines · spleen

libra — kidneys · lower back

scorpio — pelvic organs
sagittarius — hips · thighs

capricorn — knees

aquarius — calves

pisces — feet

to describe and give meaning to emotional and psychological issues largely left unanswered by rational science. However, beyond knowing their Sun sign, most people are largely unaware of the richness of these symbols and just how intricately they can describe health and disease in our bodies. The objective of this book is to introduce and explain simply the symbolic richness of the zodiac signs and show how they can be used to illuminate our experience of health in everyday life. The inner clarification that these symbols bring can be an important part of the healing process. With this objective in mind the text will provide detailed descriptions of the symbols to enhance understanding of them and help people see their validity in everyday health matters.

The type of astrology used regarding health matters and demonstrated in this book is different from the regular 'Sun signs' that most readers will be familiar with. Whilst much of the symbolism is similar to natal astrology its interpretation has a different emphasis due the symbolism being related to the event of an illness starting rather than the time of birth. Those readers who are solely familiar with their Sun sign will be able gain further insights into health and disease. However, the full potential of the knowledge contained in this book will only be apparent when charts of events of illness are studied. To this end those readers who are new to the subject of astrology I would strongly recommend Graham Boston's *Astrology – a beginner's guide* in this series, to learn how to draw up a chart and understand basic astrological terms and concepts. Alternatively if chart calculations are too daunting then they can be done for you by computer. For the committed, obtaining astrological software for your PC will be invaluable in your study. Alternatively it is often possible to obtain charts for specific times from an astrologer with a computer for a modest charge.

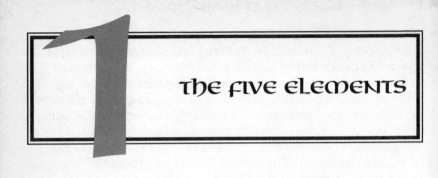

the five elements

Imagine going for a walk in the countryside on a beautiful day. The ground is soft but firm beneath your feet. The vegetation is lush. Water flows nearby. A gentle warm breeze is blowing. The sun is shining brightly from a clear blue sky. When all these factors are in harmony there is an extra magic and sparkle about the day. Nature is at her most vibrant. The intensity of the experience makes you feel relaxed, recharges your batteries and fills your heart with joy.

The simplicity and directness of this experience is the very foundation of how health has been described in medicine for thousands of years. In our depersonalised technological era, this knowledge is once again enormously valuable for making sense of our health.

How can the experience of nature at her most vibrant be used to describe health and disease in our bodies? Each component to the little visualisation of walking in the countryside can be described by means of the five Elements. Since antiquity the Elements are seen as the universal forces upon which life depends. Earth is the ground beneath our feet, from which vegetation grows. Water is the universal solvent which irrigates the soil and enables vegetation to grow. Air is the atmosphere which we breath. While Fire is the sun in the sky which provides heat, light and energy for all living organisms. Each Element is essential for life to take place. Take any one of these Elements away and life could not exist. Since these Elements are fundamental for life to occur on our planet, what more powerful tools can be found for describing the nature of life itself?

The fifth Element, Ether, is used to describe the vital force which animates the physical world. As in the initial visualisation, when Earth, Water, Air and Fire are in harmony the vital force flows abundantly through nature. It is important to clearly understand the relationship between Ether and the four physical Elements. It is analogous to the component colours of the spectrum within white light when it is shone through a prism. The reverse phenomenon also occurs, if all the component colours of the spectrum in their equal proportions are directed into another prism a single beam of white light is created. Similarly, when the four physical Elements are equally balanced, the flow of Ether is strengthened. Conversely, the more the four physical Elements are not in balance, the more the flow of Ether is weakened.

Since every living thing is dependent upon the Elements, the next step is to apply them to the human condition. This is done by considering the Elements symbolically.

The Earth Element

Consider for a few moments the solidity, stability and cohesiveness of Earth. From these qualities it is easy to see how the Earth Element represents the body, the most material part of human existence. In particular Earth represents the bones composing the skeletal system, the part of the body that endures long after the tissues have decomposed. Earth is also related to the digestive

organs, which enable the substance of the food that we eat to be transformed into the tissues of the body.

Earth can symbolise other aspects of human experience aside from the purely physical. At an emotional level, Earth describes emotional security and stability, those things that we need to possess in order to feel secure and comfortable. More specifically, Earth describes such emotions as depression, when to engage the will is as difficult as walking across a ploughed field after rain. Alternatively, Earth describes the nature of fear when, quite literally, hearts turn to stone.

Within work, Earth symbolises the rhythm and routine of the job structure. In particular, it shows the persistence and endurance required to achieve success within work. More negatively, Earth can also describe the tiredness and stagnation of our energy that frustrates the achievement of our goals.

Within mental experience Earth symbolises concentration of the mind and the intense structuring of ideas – 'building castles in the Air'. Earth describes the heaviness and rigidity of ideas that frequently occurs within law, science and tradition.

When we are healthy Earth describes the physiological phenomenon of homoeostasis, whereby the multitude of biochemical processes maintain their proper balance and function. In disease, shortage of Earth is linked to malnutrition and starvation while an excess of Earth describes obesity. Earth is linked to precipitation and blockages inside the body, whether it is the formation of blood clots in thrombosis, the blockage of the bowel in constipation or the formation of stones in the gall bladder or kidneys.

All of these levels of the temperament are interconnected, so that an excess or deficiency of any Element can have effects throughout the levels. For example, a deficiency of the Earth Element may well describe a person who is insecure and lacks emotional stability. Physically they may appear very nervous or highly strung. Their daily life is typically disorganised and they often have great difficulty 'getting their act together'. In order to compensate they may well over eat, typically having binges at times of greatest unhappiness. The excessive intake of food can, quite literally, be seen as directly

imbibing Earth into the body, to buffer their emotional state. If it is not rectified the long-term effects of this Elemental imbalance leads to obesity, where excessive weight of the body puts increasing strain on the joints of the skeletal system. The increased tissue mass places increasing demands on the circulatory system. As the circulation becomes more stagnant fatty deposits occur within the blood vessels. In time these deposits build up and increase the danger of thrombosis, where a blood clot forms and blocks the flow of blood through a blood vessel. If the blood supply to a vital organ is restricted or cut off this is often life threatening. For example, a clot blocking a blood vessel in the brain will causes a stroke.

Alternatively an excess of the Earth Element may well describe a person who is oppressed by tradition. If a person is born into a culture with a strong religious influence or political oppression, then collective fears are very common. Fear directly blocks the free expression of will causing people to become apathetic and lethargic. In relationships their sluggish emotional energy places considerable strain on their partner, who has to drag them along. The anxiety surrounding fear numbs their mind to new possibilities and gradually erodes their self-esteem. The resultant lack of confidence frequently means they neglect looking after themselves through diet, adequate exercise and proper relaxation. There is often a desperate struggle to prove themselves of value in relation to others. Unless a person learns how to break their patterns of fear, then nervous exhaustion and physical stagnation may result. Cancer frequently occurs in relation to this emotional pattern.

The Water Element

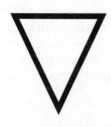

Once again consider for a few moments the fluid, receptive and mutable nature of Water. From these qualities it is easy to see how the Water Element represents emotional experience. Just as it is hard to hold water in your bare hands without it running away between your fingers, so too is it hard to define and capture specific emotions. However, if Water is used to describe the flow of emotional energy through the psyche, then individual emotions such as love, anger or fear can be visualised as different wave forms within this flow. Love is smooth and harmonious, anger is boiling and intense, while fear is stagnant and frozen.

If you imagine two drops of water touching and coalescing into a larger drop, so Water describes the medium of relationships, from the expression of love, to sexual attraction and the nurturing of children. Accordingly, within the body Water is connected to the reproductive organs, not only is Water reflected in the various sexual secretions and the menstrual cycle, but also in the embryological development of a baby unfolding within the waters of the womb. The 'breaking of the waters' essentially constitutes the start of the birth process. Water is particularly associated with fertility.

Over 70 per cent of the composition of the human body is, in fact, water. More specifically Water represents the body fluids such as blood, lymph, bile, urine and cerebrospinal fluid. The flow or circulation of blood or lymph is essentially linked to Water. Also Water is symbolically linked to the bladder and kidneys, organs responsible for the excretion of urine and regulation of the amount of fluid in the body. Similarly, Water relates to the endocrine glands and the secretion of hormones into the blood. Water relates to other secretions such as saliva and sweat. Diseases involving discharges, haemorrhage or the build up of fluid in the body are Watery.

Within work Water represents the interaction with other people. The rapport between vendors and clients. After providing a service for the client, the vendor is essentially rewarded for their time and energy with money. Money can be seen from this perspective as a unit of emotional energy. This transaction is described with an appropriate Watery metaphor – the cash flow.

Within mental experience Water is linked the imagination. Just as the surface of water reflects what ever occurs around it, so too Water symbolises the fleeting images that form in our minds. When carefully nurtured the imagination provides the gateway for the development of intuition, inner perception and spiritual unfoldment. More negatively expressed the imagination can totally overpower normal daily awareness and engulf a person in inner torment. The alienated world of the lunatic.

The interconnection of all these levels through the Water Element can be demonstrated in a relationship that is not working out. The absence of love is likely to create a lot of emotional tension. For a woman this tension can contribute to premenstrual symptoms. The resultant heavy periods and blood loss can easily lead to iron deficiency anaemia. Untreated the loss of red blood cells causes intense lethargy. As a result they may well be unable to work and derive an income. This depletion of energy can lead to a lack of vision of how to deal with the situation and cause utter despair at the thought of having to change their life in some way.

The Air Element

Now consider for a few moments the invisible, pervasive and changeable nature of Air. These qualities make the Air Element ideal to represent mental experience. The Air Element embraces the whole range of mental processes such intellect, reason, logic, thought and ideas, attitudes, wit, speech, language, communication and knowledge.

Within the body the Air Element is connected to the lungs which, quite literally, draw Air into the body to oxygenate the blood, enabling the cells to respire. Through the association of the Air Element with mental experience it is also linked to the brain and nervous system and subsequently the control and co-ordination of the body. The Air Element is also linked to the white blood cells and the immunological defences of the body.

Within emotional relationships Air relates to the space that is needed for couples to reflect and deal with issues that arise between them. Without this space to breathe one or both partners will find the situation stifling, preventing the positive growth and unfoldment of the relationship.

Within work the Air Element relates to the knowledge and skills needed to carry out a particular field of work. It especially relates to the ability to communicate this knowledge to others and effectively sell a service or product.

Again, all these levels are interconnected through the Air Element. A typical company work situation where employees are unable to have enough space of their own to work in will find their thoughts and ideas cramped and compromised by the pressure of those around them. Subsequently, their work performance is antagonised creating considerable nervous tension. This tension can easily be mediated to the lungs and affect respiration. In a situation where a person is metaphorically unable to breathe, an asthmatic attack may be precipitated. It is just the circumstance where people often smoke to try to release nervous tension.

The Fire Element

Now consider the dynamic, intense and radiant energy of the Fire Element. These qualities connect the Fire Element to the personal energy, drive and motivation of an individual. Within the body Fire particularly relates to the muscular system. The muscles translate our energy into physical movement of the body, whereby our intentions are transformed into action. More specifically, Fire connects with the red blood cells, which by carrying oxygen from the lungs to the cells throughout the body assist the tissues to respire, converting sugar from the blood into energy. Fire, especially, is linked to the heart, not only is it a muscular organ, but also its pumping action pushes the blood around the body so that the red blood cells can transport the oxygen to the tissues. Fire connects with the body heat that is generated from all the metabolic activities of the cells and particularly the contraction of the muscles. In disease, Fire is associated with fever and inflammation.

At an emotional level, Fire relates to the energy that a person directs towards emotional expression, sexual attraction and charisma. An excess of the Fire Element is associated with impatience, lust, anger and inner conflict.

Within work Fire relates to the application of energy to the job. The ability to execute necessary actions, achieve goals and objectives. Fire also relates to the physical strength needed to perform certain tasks. When work is performed creatively and positively it provides a deep inner satisfaction and pleasure. Generally, when work is accomplished with fulfilment and thoroughness it generates recognition and fame for its high quality.

Within mental experience, Fire relates to the knowledge and understanding of how best to direct energy. It relates to strategies and expertise needed to carry out work. In particular, business acumen and organisational skills, knowing when best to initiate certain actions and optimal utilisation of the time available.

The interconnection of all these levels through the Fire Element can be demonstrated in a stressful work situation. Generally, where employees have to carry out directions without being able to exercise their will, work becomes particularly frustrating and lacks creative fulfilment. They are unable to put their heart into their work.

Consequently, their frustrated energy builds up into considerable inner tension and anxiety. When this stress manifests itself through the body it can easily create problems as diverse as high blood pressure, heart attacks, digestive ulceration and impotence.

The Ether Element

Finally, the Ether Element represents the imperceptible, insensible and invisible flow of the vital force through the body. Simultaneously, this flow is also the medium of emotional experience and substance out of which ideas are created. Ether is, thus, intimately connected with the consciousness of an individual. It is the same vital force that heals and regenerates the body and is connected to a person's sexuality.

The sexual act demonstrates the quintessential relationship of the Five Elements. Earth represents the physical joining of two bodies. Water represents the love and emotional exchange between the couple. Fire represents their sexual attraction and expression. Air represents the pleasure and spiritual awareness. Ether represents the life force that flows between the couple. Resulting from the exchange of vital force, conception results in the creation of another individual through formation of new body (Earth), with a soul entering into it through the emotional body (Water), from where it expresses its desires, will and motivation (Fire) and ultimately mental unfoldment and awareness (Air).

Having covered what is symbolically linked to the Elements, health can now be described as the balance of the four Elements within a person. That is the harmony between the physical expression, emotional fulfilment, mental realisation and creative accomplishment that results in the enhancement of the flow of the vital force through the entire person. Seen from this perspective health is much more vibrant than merely the absence of physical symptoms, it is a state of existence to be continually strived for and experienced.

As the outer world of the physical Elements reflects the inner world of an individual then, generally, the more people live in harmony with nature, the happier and healthier their lives become. Failure to live in harmony with nature can lead to stress and disease within people.

With a little visualisation each of the four Elements can be seen to possess two of the following primary qualities; hot, cold, dry and moist. The Elements and their primary qualities are summarised in Table 1.1. All of these primary qualities are contained within Ether, which paradoxically possesses none of them.

Table 1.1 The Elements and their primary qualities

Fire	=	hot and dry
Air	=	hot and moist
Water	=	cold and moist
Earth	=	cold and dry

To reveal more insight into what can be described by Elemental knowledge, further visualisation of how the four Elements interact is especially useful. Of the six possible pairs, two combinations are the most compatible and sympathetic. The first pair includes the two masculine Elements Fire and Air, the Elements of combustion. Fire

needs Air to burn, while the rising heat draws more Air to the flames so creating more heat. The second pair includes the two feminine Elements, Water and Earth, the Elements of fertility. Water dissolves the solidness of the Earth Element making it more receptive and fertile, so enabling vegetation to grow.

The next two combinations are the most incompatible and antipathetic. The third pair includes the Elemental opposites of Fire and Water, the most reactive combination. Fire makes Water boil, while Water extinguishes Fire. This tends to be an explosive combination. The fourth pair includes the Elemental opposites of Air and Earth, the most inert combination. Though Earth contacts Air there is little interaction between them without the other two Elements of Fire and Water. It is a static and sterile combination.

The last two combinations are antagonistic but not as negative as the previous Elemental opposites. The fifth pair consists of Fire and Earth. Fire scorches the Earth making it parched and barren. The structure of the Earth breaks down and looses its fertility. The resultant dust from the Earth cannot sustain the Fire Element. The sixth pair consists of Air and Water. Air blowing over the Water stirs up waves so that its calm, reflective surface is lost. Similarly, Water evaporates into the Air causing fog and mist, whereby the clarity of the Air Element is lost.

The four Elements within the zodiac

The zodiacal signs are complex symbols with many aspects and associations. The Sun signs that most people are familiar with, are based upon what is called the tropical zodiac. Consider a map of the world; generally marked on it is a dotted line 23 degrees north of the

equator called the Tropic of Cancer. Similarly, another dotted line is found at 23 degrees south of the equator called the Tropic of Capricorn. This band between the Tropic of Cancer and the Tropic of Capricorn essentially forms a wide belt around the Earth's equator (see Figure 1.1). Next imagine this band being 'pushed' from the surface of the Earth and expanded into the depths of space. This 360° band as it circumscribes the Earth is divided into the twelve 30° sections that constitute the zodiacal signs forming the tropical zodiac.

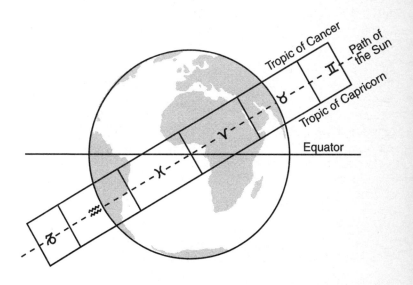

Figure 1.1 The tropical zodiac

The sequence of the zodiacal signs starts with Aries – 0° Aries is defined by the spatial position of the Sun as it crosses the equator at the vernal equinox (in the northern hemisphere) on the 23 March. The Sun is then said to have entered the sign of Aries. The remaining eleven signs of the zodiac, Taurus, Gemini, Cancer, Leo, Virgo, Libra, Scorpio, Sagittarius, Capricorn, Aquarius and Pisces all start in sequence, every 30° through out the rest of the band completing the tropical zodiac (see Figure 1.2).

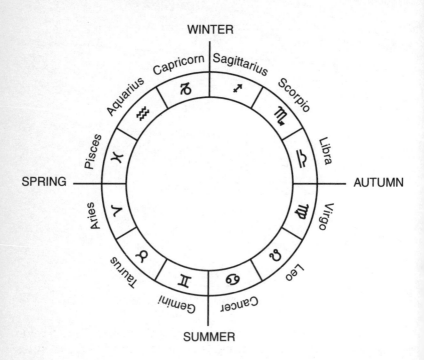

Figure 1.2 The zodiacal signs

Each zodiacal sign has an Elemental ruler, whereby it is associated with one of the Elements; Earth, Water, Air and Fire. Of the twelve signs within the zodiac three are associated with each Element. They are often referred to as the Elemental triplicities. The Elemental rulerships are outlined in Table 1.2.

Table 1.2 The Elemental triplicities

Aries is a Cardinal Fire sign

Taurus is a Fixed Earth sign

Gemini is a Mutable Air sign

Cancer is a Cardinal Water sign

Leo is a Fixed Fire sign

Virgo is a Mutable Earth sign

Libra is a Cardinal Air sign

Scorpio is a Fixed Water sign

Sagittarius is a Mutable Fire sign

Capricorn is a Cardinal Earth sign

Aquarius is a Fixed Air sign

Pisces is a Mutable Water sign

The table reveals another sequence running through it. The first sign is designated cardinal, the second is designated fixed and the third is designated mutable, and so on through the rest of the zodiacal signs. The different qualities of cardinality, fixity and mutability will be considered in the following four chapters.

Each of the Elements within the zodiac have needs central to their well being. Understanding and satisfying these needs provides a foundation with which to build health upon. Earth signs need to have security and stability. Water signs thirst for emotional fulfilment. Air signs desire expression of ideas and interests. Fire signs yearn for creative accomplishment and achievement of goals. Failure to obtain this fulfilment is profoundly stressful and can undermine health. Look at the Element of your Sun sign (and Ascendant sign if known), then consider what your needs are. For example, Aries being a Fire sign yearn creative accomplishment or Pisces being a Water sign thirsts for emotional fulfilment.

PRACTICE

Earth signs: can earth their energies through gardening, walking, rock climbing, cooking, sculpture, pottery, jewelry, yoga, massage, earth sciences. Excess Earth can be countered by breathing exercises, study, public speaking, writing, travel, Qi Gung.

Water signs: derive pleasure through relationships, music, photography, painting, fishing, nautical activities, scuba diving, healing, team work. Excess Water can be countered by swimming, dance, tai chi, aerobics.

Air signs: engage interest through intellectual pursuits, reading, writing, languages, philosophy, singing, media, communications, travel, gliding. Excess Air can be countered by breathing exercises, hatha yoga, massage, crafts, different cuisines.

Fire signs: experience satisfaction through adequate physical exercise, sport, martial arts, challenging work, performing arts, debates, definite goals, social activities, variety. Excess Fire can be countered by cold showers, sailing, surfing, relaxation exercises, yoga, meditation or artistic activities.

These lists are not exhaustive. Alternatively, consider what activities you enjoy and think about what Element it involves. Then see how it concords with the Element of your Sun sign.

THE FIRE SIGNS

A ll the Fire signs are masculine, associated with the day and are hot *and dry in nature.*

ARIES

Aries the ram is the first sign of the Fire triplicity and the first sign of the zodiac. Aries is ruled by the Planet Mars (see Figure 2.1). As a cardinal sign Aries is very strongly associated with the initiation of actions. Within the body Aries corresponds to the head and face. Indeed the glyph for Aries is thought to be analogous to the head and horns of a ram. The combination of the Fire Element propelled by the dynamic energy of Mars makes the sign particularly headstrong with a powerful need to be first at all cost. The desire to lead is linked with an intense inner drive and restlessness. Frustration of this inner drive very easily generates tensions in the head. The thwarted energy of Mars readily invokes anger leading to

rash and capricious behaviour. If this anger is expressed violently, injuries to the head are frequently sustained.

Diseases of Aries

In considering the various disease linked to each of the following zodiacal signs it is important to understand that they relate to event charts of illness. In these charts the following diseases should be considered from the corresponding sign found at the sixth house cusp or from whatever sign the Planet that rules the sixth house is located in. This will be demonstrated in Chapter 8. If your Sun is in Aries this

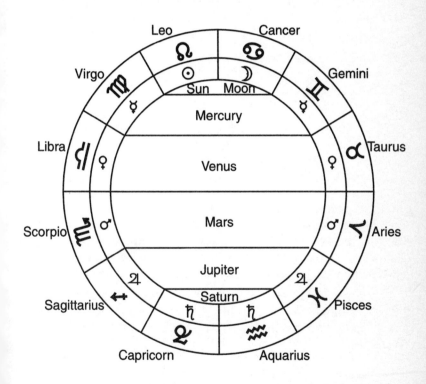

Figure 2.1 Traditional planetary rulers of the zodiac

does not necessarily mean that you will suffer from everything listed for Aries below.

The diseases of Aries are particularly focused on the head and face. From birth there may be defects to the head such as cleft palate and/or hare-lips. As a Fire sign Aries is associated with fevers generally. In particular Aries has been traditionally linked with measles, as the skin eruptions of this disease usually appear first on the face.

The generation of tension in the head means that Aries is commonly linked with headaches and migraines. Indeed, there is a vulnerability to other inflammations in the head that cause head pain such as toothache, sinusitis and earache. The latter may well be linked to vertigo, which is also linked with the sign.

The skin on the head and face is susceptible to inflammations and eruptions such as sunburn or acne. Ring-worm, a common fungal infection of sheep, located on the scalp is a traditionally associated with the sign, as is baldness.

Aries is anatomically linked to the brain and indirectly to various conditions affecting the functioning of the nervous system. These can include strokes where a thrombus or clot prevents blood from reaching vital parts of the brain. Loss of brain function can lead to immediate loss of consciousness or death. Those that survive a stroke frequently experience paralysis to one side of the face or body, loss of speech or spatial sense. Epilepsy and convulsions are also linked to the sign which may be caused by a brain tumour or trauma to the head. Similarly, conditions that effect the facial nerves such as Bell's palsy, shingles and tic doloureux can be identified here.

Associating Aries with the brain means that the sign is also linked to mental conditions such as madness, depression and catalepsy – a trance like state of psychological withdrawal found in psychotic conditions.

The intensity of the Arian inner drive may become burnt out and collapse. Paradoxically, the symptoms of lethargy and forgetfulness found with nervous exhaustion are often found with this sign.

Leo

Leo the Lion is the second sign of the Fire triplicity and the fifth sign of the zodiac. Leo is ruled by the Sun. As a fixed sign Leo is very strongly associated with pride in all their actions. Within the body Leo corresponds to the heart and back. The glyph for Leo is thought to resemble the head and tail of a lion. The combination of the Fire Element focused by the creative energy of the Sun makes the sign very self-centred. When this energy is expressed positively it can create the charismatic leader. Where the Leonine creative energy is blocked by having to execute other's instructions rather than their own ambitions they become vulnerable to heart attacks.

Diseases of Leo

The diseases of Leo predominantly involve the heart. Most seriously, occlusion of the cardiac arteries by a thrombus or blood clot causing a heart attack. The nervous tension of Leo can be linked with palpitations and arhythmias affecting the heart. As a Fire sign Leo is

also associated with fevers generally. In particular, it is linked to pericarditis and rheumatic heart disease, febrile conditions that directly involve the heart. Conditions that cause pain to radiate to the ribs and back such as pleurisy have been linked to Leo. Through the Fire Element Leo is linked to the formation of bile by the liver. Consequently, it is linked to jaundice where the normal bile secretion is blocked, causing an abnormal build up of bile pigments in the blood which stain the skin yellow. As the Sun is a co-ruler of the eyes, Leo is also linked to inflammations of the eyes. Leo is traditionally a barren sign.

SAGITTARIUS ♐

Sagittarius the archer is the third sign of the Fire triplicity and the ninth sign of the zodiac. Sagittarius is ruled by Jupiter. As a mutable sign, Sagittarius describes the Fire Element at it most expansive. Sagittarius is known for its tremendous enthusiasm as it radiates its energy in all directions. The glyph for Sagittarius is thought to allude to the bow and arrow of the archer. Within the body Sagittarius corresponds to the hips and thighs.In its thirst for new horizons the Sagittarian energy enjoys travel, challenges and sport.

Diseases of Sagittarius

The diseases of Sagittarius particularly involve the hips and thighs. Injury to the hips and thighs through sport is a common association, especially equestrian activities. The pain of sciatica has long been

identified with this sign. The Jupiterian rulership may well lead the Sagittarian to over indulgence in rich food and drink. A particular consequence may well be arthritis affecting the hip joints. Like the other Fire signs Sagittarius is also associated with fevers generally.

3 THE EARTH SIGNS

All the Earth signs are feminine, associated with the night and are cold and dry in nature.

TAURUS

Taurus the bull is the first sign of the Earth triplicity and the second sign of the zodiac. Taurus is ruled by the planet Venus. As a fixed sign Taurus is very strongly associated with the consolidation of material objects. Within the body Taurus corresponds to the neck and throat. Indeed the glyph for Taurus is thought to be analogous to the neck and shoulders of a bull. The combination of the Earth Element with the sensual enjoyment of Venus makes the sign particularly fond of food.

Diseases of Taurus

The diseases of Taurus are chiefly focused on the throat. They include a number of inflammatory conditions affecting the particular organs such as laryngitis, pharyngitis and tracheitis. A corresponding lymphadenitis or swelling of the lymph nodes is likely to accompany these inflammations. In particular, tonsillitis is connected here to Taurus. Venus is linked to the formation of phlegm which is often a symptom of inflammations in the throat. Dairy foods are thought to cause excessive phlegm and to aggravate inflammations of the throat. Goitre or enlargement of the thyroid gland is also linked to the sign.

VIRGO

Virgo the virgin is the second sign of the Earth triplicity and the sixth sign of the zodiac. Virgo is ruled by the planet Mercury. As a mutable sign Virgo is very strongly associated with the analysis and organisation of material objects. Within the body Virgo corresponds to the spleen and intestines. The latter is responsible for the breaking down of food into its constituent molecules for absorption into the body. The glyph for Virgo can be seen to allude to a virgin standing with her sheaf of corn beside her. The combination of the Earth Element with the inquisitiveness of Mercury makes the sign particularly critical and fussy of material things. There is a lot of nervous energy generated through worrying about ideals. This nervous tension is very easily directed to the intestines upsetting their normal harmonious function.

Diseases of Virgo

The diseases of Virgo especially involve the intestines. Nervous tension mediated to the bowel can cause the symptoms that characterise irritable bowel syndrome. These include wind, constipation or diarrhoea, sharp colic pain, mucus and bleeding. These symptoms may well be aggravated by gluten, the sticky protein present in wheat and other grains. Stagnation of the bowels may be linked to candida colonisation of the intestines. Virgo is especially linked to depression, which is often related to constipation. In later life, Virgo can highlight tumours which cause intestinal obstruction. Parasites such as intestinal worms are shown here. Virgo is also linked to conditions involving the spleen, especially those where it becomes hard and enlarged. Virgo is another barren sign of the zodiac.

CAPRICORN

Capricorn the goat is the third sign of the Earth triplicity and the tenth sign of the zodiac. Capricorn is ruled by Saturn. As a cardinal Earth sign, Capricorn is particularly associated with planning and designing material projects. Within the body Capricorn corresponds to the knees and bones. The glyph for Capricorn is thought to describe the emerging sea-goat. The combination of the Earth Element concentrated by the influence of Saturn makes the sign the most disciplined and resourceful of the Earth signs. However, the Capricornian energy is very susceptible to fear. Fear can block their motivation and create an attitude of self-denial which is particularly destructive to their achievements.

Diseases of Capricorn

The knees of Capricorn are particularly prone to injuries and sprains. The bones are liable to fracture and dislocation. Capricorn is vulnerable to skin conditions where there is a build up of hard skin. Of all the Earth signs Capricorn suffers the most from depression and melancholy. The sign has been noted for hard painless swellings in the body.

THE AIR SIGNS

All the Air signs are masculine, associated with the day and are hot and moist in nature.

GEMINI

Gemini the twins is the first sign of the Air triplicity and the third sign of the zodiac. Gemini is ruled by the planet Mercury. As a mutable sign Gemini delights seeking out new ideas, opinions and interests and then sharing them with others. Within the body Gemini corresponds to the shoulders, arms and hands. The glyph for Gemini is the Roman numeral for two, which is analogous to the two bodies of the twins. Traditionally one twin is male, the other female. With the ruling Planet Mercury representing Ether the vital force, Gemini was a sign particularly connected with sexuality. Consequently the twins have been depicted as having sexual intercourse. The combination of the Air Element with the inquisitiveness of Mercury makes the sign prone to anxiety and

worry. The preoccupation with mental pursuits can make Gemini negligent of having adequate, food, sleep and exercise. An intense social life can often lead to physical exhaustion.

Diseases of Gemini

The diseases of Gemini especially involve the hands, arms and shoulders. This can be due to accidents causing fractures and dislocations. Formerly Gemini was linked to diseases caused by blood letting at the wrists and seen to cause corruption of the blood. The contemporary counterpart must be diseases due to taking drugs intravenously, with all the attendant risks of infection and embolism. Gemini is associated with sexual problems, formerly described as 'distempered fancies'. Gemini is also a barren sign.

Libra

Libra the scales is the second sign of the Air triplicity and the seventh sign of the zodiac. Libra is ruled by the planet Venus. As a cardinal sign Libra enjoys initiating new ideas. Within the body Libra corresponds to the kidneys and lower back. The glyph for Libra is analogous to a pair of scales. The combination of the Air Element with the love of Venus makes the sign seek balance, harmony and resolution to conflict. The principle role of the kidneys is to excrete metabolic waste in the urine, however in performing this role they need to maintain the water, electrolyte and acid-base balance of the blood. Disease of the kidneys can seriously disrupt their function and become life threatening.

Diseases of Libra

The diseases of Libra predominantly involve the kidneys. This can involve serious inflammatory conditions such as pyelonephritis and glomerulonephritis. Kidney stones or gravel may be shown here as they are a frequently linked to kidney infections. The intense pain from the kidney is referred to the lower back. 'Corruption of the blood' has traditionally been linked to Libra which would well explain impaired kidney function.

Aquarius

Aquarius the water carrier is the third sign of the Air triplicity and the eleventh sign of the zodiac. Aquarius is ruled by the planet Saturn. As a fixed sign Aquarius enjoys defining ideas and principles. Within the body Aquarius corresponds to the calves and ankles. The glyph for Aquarius is analogous to a pair of air waves, symbolising the transmission of ideas. The combination of the Air Element with the structure of Saturn makes the sign seek out the principles and laws that govern all things. Negatively expressed this mental energy can be very dogmatic and iconoclastic. Emotional relationships are often very difficult for Aquarius.

Diseases of Aquarius

The diseases of Aquarius predominantly involve disease occurring in the legs and ankles. This is commonly the result of poor circulation of the blood and can include symptoms such as cramps and swelling around the ankle. Intermittent claudication or 'window shopper's disease' is particularly linked here. Like the other Air signs Aquarius is linked to disorders that upset the harmonious functioning of the blood. Sciatic pain may well be referred to the calves and ankles.

5 THE WATER SIGNS

All the Water signs are feminine, associated with the night and are cold and moist in nature.

CANCER

Cancer the crab is the first sign of the Water triplicity and the fourth sign of the zodiac. Cancer is ruled by the Moon. As a cardinal Water sign, Cancer is particularly associated with defending their own emotional space. Within the body Cancer corresponds to the chest, breast, liver and stomach. Indeed, the glyph for Cancer is thought to be analogous to the two breasts. The combination of the Water Element with the influence of the Moon makes the sign exceptionally vulnerable to changes of mood. Like the other Water signs Cancer is described as mute, creating a secretive nature that has difficulty sharing ideas with others. Regarding fertility, Cancer along with the other Water signs are fruitful.

Diseases of Cancer

The diseases of Cancer specifically affect the breast, chest, stomach or liver. These can include inflammations such as mastitis in the breast, pleurisy affecting the pleural lining of the chest wall, gastritis in the stomach and hepatitis in the liver. The sign is linked to phlegmatic conditions of the chest associated with coughing. The stomach can have excess cold with poor appetite and weak digestion or excess heat with acidity and ulceration. However, due to the powerful influence the Moon has on the body, Cancer is also related to diseases that effect the whole body. These include diseases that cause excess fluid or oedema in the body. Due to gravity, excess fluid may accumulate around the ankles. Cancer is the sign especially related to the phenomenon of cancer generally in the body. It is interesting that the most common cancers occur specifically in parts of the body linked to either the sign Cancer or to the Moon. These are the breast, lung and stomach, along with lymphatic and haematological systems.

SCORPIO

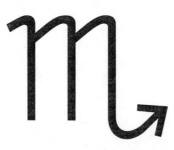

Scorpio the scorpion is the second sign of the Water triplicity and the eighth sign of the zodiac. Scorpio is ruled by the planet Mars. As a fixed Water sign, Scorpio is particularly known for emotional intensity. Within the body Scorpio is linked to the sexual organs and the pelvic area. The barb on the glyph for Scorpio is thought to be analogous to the penis. The combination of the Water Element with

the dynamism of Mars makes the sign prone to harbouring strong passions and resentment. Coupled with the mute quality of the Water signs this can lead to emotional outbursts that others find hard to understand. Scorpio is strongly linked to sexuality and is a fruitful sign.

Diseases of Scorpio

The diseases of Scorpio specifically affect the bladder, anus and sexual organs. Scorpio is commonly linked to cystitis or inflammation of the bladder arising from infections in the urinary tract. Similarly, gravel and stone in the bladder that can accompany a chronic urinary infection is shown here. Additionally, conditions that affect the passing of water are also linked. This can be difficulty in voiding urine as in strangury or an enlarged prostate. Alternatively, this may be excess urinary production as in various forms of diabetes or incontinence. The link of Scorpio generally to the pelvic area includes such conditions as inguinal hernias, anal fistulas and piles. All venereal diseases are encompassed in Scorpio including gonorrhoea and syphilis. Similarly, all gynaecological problems in women are shown here including pelvic inflammatory disease.

PISCES

Pisces the fishes is the third sign of the Water triplicity and the twelfth sign of the zodiac. Pisces is ruled by the planet Jupiter. As a mutable Water sign, Pisces is particularly known for emotional

dissipation. Within the body the two fishes of Pisces are linked to the two feet. The glyph of Pisces depicts two fishes, one swimming upwards, the other swimming downwards joined by a central belt. It is said to represent the dilemma of the soul in deciding between spiritual aspiration and material fulfilment. The combination of the Water Element with the expansiveness of Jupiter gives considerable emotional depth to the sign. This depth is at the expense of a strong physical vitality. Pisces has a long reputation as a weak sickly sign. Despite this Pisces is still one of the fruitful signs.

Diseases of Pisces

The diseases of Pisces are focused upon the feet. These include lameness, aches and diseases such as arthritis, gout and chilblains. Like the other Water signs Pisces is linked to phlegmatic conditions such as colds and bronchitis. In former times, when footwear was poor, Pisces was traditionally linked to diseases that 'come by catching wet and cold at the feet'. The skin is vulnerable to irritations, allergies and eruptions.

6

ThE SEVEN
TRADITIONAL
PLANETS

The energy of each planet is expressed differently through each of the zodiacal signs. The planetary energy is expressed most powerfully when it is present in the sign of its rulership, where it is described as dignified (see Figure 2.1). Conversely, the planetary energy is expressed weakly when it is present in the sign opposite to the one that it rules, where it is described as in detriment. A planet can also have an affinity with a particular sign where, once again, the planetary energy is expressed powerfully, though they do not actually rule the sign. This sign is called its exaltation. Conversely, the planetary energy is expressed weakly when it is present in the opposite sign to its exaltation, where it is described as in its fall.

SUN

The Sun is dignified in Leo, the sign of its rulership. It is in detriment in Aquarius, the opposite sign to Leo. The Sun is exalted in Aries while

having its fall in Libra. The nature of the Sun is hot and dry making it accord with the Fire Element and the signs of the Fire triplicity.

The Sun chiefly rules the heart and arteries and, consequently, the circulation of blood through the arterial system. Traditionally, the heart is the seat of the soul. The soul is also ruled by the Sun and visualised as the source of light within each person from where their vital force is generated. For just as the Sun in the heavens provides light and energy for all living creatures, so the Sun within our hearts provides the vital force that sustains our bodies. The vital force flows within the blood and is thereby circulated around the body.

The Sun, along with the Moon, rules the eyes and, consequently, the sense of vision. More specifically, the Sun traditionally rules the right eye of a man and the left eye of woman.

Solar diseases

Like the zodical signs, in considering the various diseases linked to each of the following planets again it is important to understand they relate to event charts of illness. In these charts the following diseases should be considered from the planet that rules the sixth house. The tables that follow specifically relate to the diseases found when the planet that rules the sixth house is located in each of the zodiacal signs in turn. Do not, therefore, conceive of these tables as a shopping list of all that can or will go wrong in your body. It is the illness charts that determine which part of these lists are relevant. This will be demonstrated in Chapter 8.

The diseases associated with the Sun relate very specifically to the heart and encompass the whole range of cardiac problems, from palpitations to cardiac arrest. A number of circulatory symptoms are also linked with the Sun such as cramps, fainting, high or low blood pressure and headaches.

Similarly, the Sun is linked to diseases of the eyes, from the problems of vision like long- or short-sightedness to the swelling of ophthalmia.

Through the link with the Fire Element diseases of the Sun are linked to an excess or deficiency of this Element in the body. Accordingly, the Sun is linked to various fevers, conditions that traditionally were seen as an excess of choleric humour. The word choleric comes from the Greek word *chole* meaning bile. The Sun is thereby linked to other diseases effecting the formation and secretion of bile, such as jaundice.

Table 6.1 Diseases associated with the Sun in particular signs

---

Sun in Aries
Conjunctivitis, ophthalmia, migraine, headache, fainting, swooning, acne on the face, halitosis, fevers, pains and weakness in the thighs.

Sun in Taurus
Arthritis and swelling in the knees, tonsillitis, pharyngitis, peritonsillar abscess, swollen lymph nodes of the neck.

Sun in Gemini
Excess heat in the blood, epidemic fevers, skin eruptions over whole body, scurvy, pains and weakness in legs.

Sun in Cancer
Measles, chest infections, fevers associated with catarrh and coughs, pleurisy, hyperacidity, gastric ulceration, jaundice, hoarseness, dropsy, pains and weakness in knees, shoulders and arms.

Sun in Leo
High blood pressure, violent pains in the head, madness, heartburn, gall stone, pains in the back, thyphus.

Sun in Virgo
Gastric tumours, diarrhoea, dysentery, tonsillitis, pharyngitis and swellings in the neck.

Sun in Libra
Excess heat in the blood, high blood pressure, anginal pain in the arms and shoulders, kidney stones and gravel, syphilis.

Sun in Scorpio
Pelvic inflammatory disease, cystitis, burning urine, gastric tumours, chest pain.

Sun in Sagittarius
Arthritis in the hips, sciatic pain in the thighs, anal fistula, fevers, swooning, diseases of the heart and intestines.

Sun in Capricorn:
Arthritis in the knees, lameness, indigestion, fevers.

Sun in Aquarius
Excess heat in the blood, shock, palpitations, skin eruptions, kidney disease, including gravel or stone, strangury.

Sun in Pisces
Pelvic inflammatory disease, inflammation of the genital organs, strangury, burning pains arising from pelvic area.

MOON

The Moon is dignified in Cancer, the sign of its rulership. It is in detriment in Capricorn, the opposite sign to Cancer. The Moon is exalted in Taurus while having its fall in Scorpio. The nature of the Moon is cold and moist making it accord with the Water Element and the signs of the Water triplicity.

The Moon notably rules the brain and consequently has a powerful influence over the functioning of the nervous system. In contrast to the Sun, which is linked to the generation of the vital force in the heart, the Moon enhances the circulation of vital force through the blood around the body. The Moon is linked to the stomach, bowels and the rhythms of digestion. The Moon is also linked to the bladder with its cyclic filling and emptying.

The Moon, along with the Sun, rules the eyes and, consequently, the sense of vision. More specifically, the Moon traditionally rules the left eye of a man and the right eye of woman.

Lunar diseases

In general, the Lunar characteristics of disease are cold and moist, so that the body lacks heat and energy while prone to increased catarrhal secretions. The patient is lethargic and lacks vitality.

The diseases associated with the Moon relate to the brain and involve a spectrum of neurological disorders such as strokes, epilepsy or falling sickness, convulsions, vertigo, paralysis and loss of sensation. The Moon is traditionally associated with diseases specifically affecting the left side of the body. Strokes causing damage to the right side of the brain are frequently linked to paralysis of the left side of the body. Traditionally, the Moon is also linked to lunacy as the period of predominant mental and emotional unrest occurs at the full Moon.

Through the sign of Cancer, the Moon chiefly rules the stomach, in particular it is associated with a cold stomach and surfeits. The Moon being cold and moist. A cold stomach lacks the fire of gastric secretion consequently digestion is slow and absorption is poor, creating the sensation of having over eaten.

The Moon is linked to a number of diseases affecting the bowels, such as colic where the intense spasmodic pain waxes and wanes. The Moon is also linked to diarrhoea, which can be seen as too much water affecting the digestive system. Interestingly, the Moon is also traditionally linked to intestinal worms. This association has most probably been made through the observation that parasitic threadworms migrate to the anus to lay their eggs at night time, when they cause the most intense itching.

The Moon is very specifically linked to the bladder, hence the Moon is related to inflammation and kidney stones. The Moon is also, with the Sun, linked to diseases of the eyes. In particular, it is linked to conjunctivitis, discharges and injuries to the eyes.

The Moon is linked to body fluids generally, along with various excretions and discharges such as urine, mucus and sweat. Lunar disease is often linked with either excessive or deficient body fluids or secretions. Similarly, since the Moon is specifically linked to the monthly cycle of menstruation, Lunar diseases include the absence or excessive menstrual blood flow. The rhythmic occurrence of premenstrual symptoms is especially linked to the Moon.

Table 6.2 Diseases associated with the Moon in particular signs

> **Moon in Aries**
> Convulsions, sinusitis, catarrhal conditions of the ear and nose, measles, lethargy, weakness in the eyes, arthritic pains in the knees.
>
> **Moon in Taurus**
> Pains in the legs and feet, oedema or swelling in the body, measles, tonsillitis, pharyngitis and catarrhal conditions of the throat.
>
> **Moon in Gemini**
> Gout in the hands and feet, rheumatoid arthritis, excessive food intake, swellings and obstructions in the body.

Moon in Cancer
Indigestion, gastric disorders, excessive food intake, convulsions and epilepsy, oedema or swelling in the body, ascites, dropsy, measles, conditions of the breast.

Moon in Leo
Low blood pressure, congestive heart failure, tonsillitis, pharyngitis, peritonsillar abscess, gastric reflux and heartburn.

Moon in Virgo
Obstructions, swellings and pain in the intestines, poor circulation, swellings and weakness in the arms and shoulders.

Moon in Libra
Kidney disorders, lower back pain, wind and intestinal spasm, leucorrhoea, thrush, excessive food intake, pleurisy.

Moon in Scorpio
Discharges and inflammation of the sexual organs, thrush, congestive heart failure, dropsy, poisoning, coma, gastric disorders.

Moon in Sagittarius
Lameness, weakness in the thighs, sciatica, intestinal disorders, indigestion.

Moon in Capricorn
Kidney or gall stones, weak, hyperflexible back, arthritis and swelling of the knees, leucorrhoea, thrush.

Moon in Aquarius
Hysteria, swelling and pains in the legs, ankles and sexual organs.

Moon in Pisces
Cold feet, poor circulation, gout in the feet, rheumatoid arthritis, swelling in the legs, dropsies, anaemia.

SATURN

Saturn is dignified in Capricorn and Aquarius, the signs of its rulership. It is in detriment in Cancer and Leo, the opposite signs to Capricorn and Aquarius respectively. Saturn is exalted in Libra while having its fall in Aries. The nature of Saturn is cold and dry making it accord with the Earth Element and the signs of the Earth triplicity.

Saturn specifically rules all the bones that comprise the skeletal system and constitutes the foundation of the bodily tissues. The teeth are similarly linked to Saturn. Of the bodily organs Saturn rules the spleen. Saturn is linked to the ears generally and is consequently linked with hearing and balance. In particular, Saturn is traditionally said to rule the right ear, in contrast to Mars which rules the left ear.

SATURNINE DISEASES

In general, the Saturnine characteristics of disease are cold and dry, so that the body lacks heat and vitality. The diminished vital force means the body is often unable to resolutely overcome the disease, which consequently endures in the body and progressively debilitates it. The disease may ultimately be the cause of death. Such an illness is called chronic after the Greek name for Saturn – *Kronos*.

The diseases associated with Saturn particularly relate to the spleen, such as the enlargement that occurs with liver damage. Saturn is linked to such diseases that affect the bones and teeth such as fractures, dislocations, toothache and pain in the bones from tumours

or arthritis. Saturn is associated with deafness, vertigo and tinnitus or ringing in the ears. More specifically, all impediments in the right ear.

Saturn relates to blockages and obstructions in the body. Within the digestive system Saturn is linked to constipation and its frequent consequence, haemorrhoids. When the bowels are not excreting properly skin eruptions frequently occur, again linked to Saturn. Constipation of the bowel is often linked to a non-specific depression. Depression in turn causes the bowel function to slow down and become more stagnant.

Within the blood Saturn specifically relates to the clotting mechanism and the formation of blood clots or thrombi. Consequently, Saturn is linked to strokes and heart attacks, along with the attendant complications of paralysis and loss of control of the bodily functions.

Within the lungs Saturn causes the secretion of phlegm to become thick and tenacious. This can significantly obstruct the airways making breathing laboured and difficult. Saturn is thereby linked to asthma, chronic bronchitis and pneumonia.

Within the kidneys Saturn is linked to the formation of kidney stones. There is a strong connection between loss of calcium salts from the bones, causing their weakening and the formation of stones in the kidney. Depending on the size of the stones, the kidneys can become seriously blocked. Poor excretion of waste products links Saturn with gout and arthritis.

Emotionally, Saturn is linked with fear. The impact of fear can have many forms from the trembling and shaking caused by the nervous system in shock, to the more delayed apathy and depression of motivation. Intense fear causes the mind to become numb and unable to see any way out of the situation. People become reluctant to speak and communicate their difficulties with others. The blockage to their will power means that they become petrified, quite literally 'turned to stone'. Through fear the flow of vital force through the body becomes blocked causing severe lassitude and weariness. When this happens the effects of existing disease on the body is compounded. In this state the body is vulnerable to the formation of cancer and immuno-deficient diseases. The depression of the vital force with Saturn also links it to impotence.

Table 6.3 Diseases associated with Saturn in particular signs

Saturn in Aries
Depression, congested sinuses, colds, gastric tumours, cold stomach, toothache, deafness.

Saturn in Taurus
Chronic infections and swelling in the neck and throat, laryngitis, hoarseness, whooping cough, cold stomach, gout, scurvy, depression.

Saturn in Gemini
Fractures and diseases affecting the arms and shoulders, paralysis, wasting diseases, septicaemia, pleurisy, intestinal spasm.

Saturn in Cancer
Chronic lung infections, bronchitis, asthma, bronchiectasis, lung cancer, whooping cough, chronic mastitis and abscess in the breasts, scanty milk production, breast cancer, anorexia, scurvy.

Saturn in Leo
Heart afflicted by grief or poison, cardiac arrest, nephrosis, weakness and pains in the back, liver cirrhosis, jaundice, nervous afflictions, hiatus hernia.

Saturn in Virgo
Low blood pressure and poor circulation, griping, constipation, bowel tumours, weakness in the thighs, kidney stone and blockage of urine, depression.

Saturn in Libra
Kidney inflammations and blockage, kidney stones, glomerulonephritis, uraemia, strangury, back pain, pains in the knees and thighs, rheumatism, sciatica, gout.

Saturn in Scorpio
Swelling and inflammations of the sexual organs, pain in the bladder, inguinal hernia, piles, anal fistula, paralysis, tumours in the groin, gout in the hands and feet, depression.

Saturn in Sagittarius
Chronic arthritis in hips, weakness and injury to hips and thighs, sciatica, gout.

Saturn in Capricorn
Chronic arthritis in knees, gout in the feet, congested and painful sinuses, rheumatic disorders.

Saturn in Aquarius
Head pain and toothache, ear infections, inflammation of eustachian tubes and middle ear, sore throat, deafness, arthritic pain in the joints, bruises, poor circulation, cramps, swelling in the legs.

Saturn in Pisces
Chronic catarrhal conditions, arthritis or gout in the feet and toes, poor circulation, dropsy, ME.

JUPITER

♃

Jupiter is dignified in Sagittarius and Pisces, the signs of its rulership. It is in detriment in Gemini and Virgo, the opposite signs to Sagittarius and Pisces respectively. Jupiter is exalted in Cancer while having its fall in Capricorn. The nature of Jupiter is hot and moist making it accord with the Air Element and the signs of the Air triplicity.

Jupiter specifically rules the lungs, along with ribs and sides of the chest. The expansion of the chest and lungs draws the Air Element inside the body and into the blood. The liver, the largest bodily organ, located underneath the ribs on the right-hand side of the body, is also ruled by Jupiter. The liver has an important role in regulating the blood chemistry. Traditionally, Jupiter's role in the liver is to preserve the correct composition of the blood, thereby enhancing the flow of vital force around the body. Jupiter thus is connected to the blood and its circulation around the body through the various blood vessels. In particular, Jupiter is linked to the transportation of oxygen from the Air Element to the tissues, so that they can respire. The importance of this vital function is highlighted by the fact that should the brain cells become deprived of oxygen they die in a matter of minutes. The hot and moist nature of Jupiter links it to the many digestive processes of the gastro-intestinal tract.

Jupiterian Diseases

In general, the Jupiterian characteristics of disease are hot and moist, creating an abundance of heat and vitality in the body. For this reason, though Jupiterian diseases may be severe, they are relatively short lived. Afterwards people often feel much fitter and healthier than they have done for a long time.

The diseases associated with Jupiter particularly relate to the lungs and includes inflammation such as pneumonia and its attendant symptoms of excessive phlegm, haemoptysis or coughing up blood, difficulty breathing and inflammation of the pleura or pleurisy.

Liver disease is particularly associated with Jupiter such as hepatitis, cirrhosis and jaundice along with all the accompanying effects on both the blood and digestion. Jupiter is associated with symptoms of poor circulation such as oedema or swelling, cramps, intense itching of the skin and infective conditions of the blood such as septicaemia, toxaemia and pyaemia.

Since Jupiter normally enhances the flow of vital force around the body through the blood while we are asleep, diseases that compromise the influence of Jupiter may well lead to a tiredness that

no amount of sleep can ease. On waking people still feel like a zombie, dragging a dead body around.

Table 6.4 Diseases associated with Jupiter in particular signs

Jupiter in Aries
High blood pressure, headache, stroke, fainting, swooning, brain tumour, laryngitis, peritonsillar abscess, goitre, strange dreams and imaginations.

Jupiter in Taurus
Inflammation and swelling in the throat, peritonsillar abscess, flatulence, spasms and griping of the bowels, gout in the hands.

Jupiter in Gemini:
Lung infections, pleurisy, hepatitis, jaundice, high blood pressure.

Jupiter in Cancer
Excessive food intake, indigestion, gastritis, food poisoning, excess fluid in the body, dropsy, lymphadenitis, lymphoedema, catarrhal conditions, scurvy.

Jupiter in Leo
Fever, lung infections, pleurisy, haemoptysis, high blood pressure, palpitations, heartburn, intestinal colic, pain in the spine.

Jupiter in Virgo
Lung infections, pneumonia or congestion of the lungs, gall stones, liver cirrhosis, enlargement of liver and spleen, flatulence, weakness in the back, depression.

Jupiter in Libra
High blood pressure, thrombosis, renal hypertension, uraemia, fevers, excessive food intake, piles, inflammation or tumours throughout the body.

Jupiter in Scorpio
Cystitis, haematuria or blood in the urine, strangury, gravel, piles, impotence, frigidity, lymphoedema, dropsy, scurvy.

Jupiter in Sagittarius
High blood pressure, fevers, septicaemia, tumours, arthritis in knees, headaches, anginal pain.

Jupiter in Capricorn
Depression, swellings or tumours obstructing the throat, goitre, peritonsillar abscess.

Jupiter in Aquarius
High blood pressure, haemorrhage, septicaemia, fleeting pains throughout the body, lumbago.

Jupiter in Pisces
Lymphoedema, leukaemia, Hodgkin's disease, Cushing's syndrome or swelling in the face, dropsy.

MARS

Mars is dignified in Aries and Scorpio, the signs of its rulership. It is in detriment in Libra and Taurus, the opposite signs to Aries and Scorpio respectively. Mars is exalted in Capricorn while having its fall in Cancer. The nature of Mars is hot and dry making it accord with the Fire Element and the signs of the Fire triplicity.

Mars very specifically rules the gall bladder, the small sac like organ which stores the bile formed by the liver and excretes it into the duodenum during digestion. Mars, like Saturn, is connected with the ears, in particular the left ear. Mars also rules the male sexual organs including the penis and testicles.

Martian diseases

In general the Martian characteristics of disease are hot and dry, generating an excessive heat which debilitates the vitality of the body. Martian diseases frequently involve intense fevers with profuse sweating that generates a considerable thirst. Similarly, Mars is linked to the burning pain of inflammation either from trauma or infection. In contrast to Saturn, Martian disease is acute. It either resolves easily with the patient making a quick recovery or it can progress rapidly to being fatal.

The diseases associated with Mars specifically relate to the gall bladder, such as when it is inflamed as in cholecystitis or blocked by gall stones as in cholelithiasis. These conditions frequently cause blockage of the flow of bile into the duodenum resulting in jaundice.

Emotionally Mars is linked with anger. Anger building up within a person can generate considerable nervous tension leading to rash and frenzied behaviour. If this tension is suppressed it can cause high blood pressure, headaches, ulcers and gall bladder disease. Should this tension be expressed violently then physical injury to the body can occur, as traditionally Mars is linked to 'all hurts by iron and fire'. Mars is thus linked to burns, blisters, wounds and scars. Mars also specifically relates to inflammatory diseases affecting the male genitals. Mars is linked to eruptive skin disorders such as shingles, acne and psoriasis, while traditionally Mars was also linked to St Anthony's fire, a condition caused by ergot poisoning.

Table 6.5 Diseases associated with Mars in particular signs

> **Mars in Aries**
> Migraines, violent head pain, meningitis, accidents and trauma to the head, conjunctivitis, acne rosacea, ringworm.
>
> **Mars in Taurus**
> Painful inflammation of throat and neck, tonsillitis, pharyngitis, kidney infections, gravel, glomerulonephritis, pyelonephritis.

Mars in Gemini
Fever, excess heat in the blood, eczema or dermatitis, acne, itches and irritations, excessive food intake, gastric acidity, inflammation and injury to arms and shoulders, inflammations of sexual organs, strangury or painful urination.

Mars in Cancer
Mastitis, gastritis, bilious attacks, dry cough, anaemia, tumours in the thighs, accidents to the feet.

Mars in Leo
Tachycardia, carditis, rheumatic heart disease, palpitations, fever, gravel in the kidneys, arthritic pain in the knees.

Mars in Virgo
Fever, colic, gastroenteritis, food poisoning, intestinal tumours, dysentery, worms in children, varicose veins.

Mars in Libra
Fever, kidney disease, glomerulonephritis, pyelonephritis, gravel, burning urine, leucorrhoea.

Mars in Scorpio
Venereal disease, ulceration of sexual organs, cystitis, dysuria, strangury, gravel, fistulas, headaches, menorrhagia, conjunctivitis.

Mars in Sagittarius
Arthritis in the hips, ulceration on legs or thighs, varicose veins, ringworm, extreme heat and dryness in the mouth or throat.

Mars in Capricorn
Arthritis in the knees, lameness, swellings in arms or hands, gout.

Mars in Aquarius
Excess heat in the blood, intermittent claudication, pains in the legs, excessive food intake, intermittent fevers.

Mars in Pisces
Arthritis in the feet, lameness, dropsy, heart failure, pulmonary oedema.

VENUS

Venus is dignified in Taurus and Libra, the signs of its rulership. It is in detriment in Aries and Scorpio, the opposite signs to Taurus and Libra respectively. Venus is exalted in Pisces while having its fall in Virgo. The nature of Venus is cold and moist making it accord with the Water Element and the signs of the Water triplicity.

Venus predominantly rules the female reproductive organs including the vagina, uterus, fallopian tubes and ovaries. Since motherhood is strongly linked with Venus the breasts, normally ruled by the Moon, during lactation are also linked to Venus. In men Venus is linked to the formation of semen.

Through the association of Taurus, Venus is also linked to the throat. Similarly through the association of Libra, Venus rules the kidneys.

Venusian diseases

In general, the Venusian characteristics of disease are cold and moist, so that the body is prone to increased catarrhal secretions.

The diseases associated with Venus particularly relate to the womb and encompass a wide range of gynaecological problems from infections such as salpingitis to uterine prolapse. Venus in particularly relates to sexually transmitted diseases formerly described as venereal disease since they were considered to be caused by an 'inordinate love of lust'. These include gonorrhoea, syphilis and genital herpes.

In men Venus is also linked to venereal diseases affecting the male sexual organs. Additionally, Venus is linked to priapism – the persistent painful erection of the penis – and impotence.

Venus is associated with diseases of the kidneys, from inflammations such as pyelonephritis to incontinence or the involuntary discharge of urine. Diabetes has long been associated with Venus as not only is copious urine produced but also excessive sugar is excreted in the urine, making it sweet to taste. This was identified in the days when doctors used to taste urine! Sugar is linked to Venus.

Table 6.6 Diseases associated with Venus in particular signs

Venus in Aries
Hydrocephalus, rhinitis, catarrhal congestion of ear and nose, sinusitis, lethargy, kidneys inflamed.

Venus in Taurus
Colds, influenza, lymphadenitis or swollen lymph nodes on the neck, catarrh in throat, venereal disease.

Venus in Gemini
Catarrh in throat, lymphoedema, dropsy, ulcerative colitis.

Venus in Cancer
Asthma, cold stomach, catarrh in stomach, poor digestion, excessive food intake.

Venus in Leo
Ill affection of the heart, intestinal colic, pains in the legs.

Venus in Virgo
Intestinal inflammation, diarrhoea, mucus colitis, pain in the sexual organs, worms in children.

Venus in Libra
Gonorrhoea, excessive intake of food or drink, flatulence, biliousness.

Venus in Scorpio
Venereal disease, pain in the sexual organs.

Venus in Sagittarius
Arthritis in the hips, gout, excessive food intake, catarrhal conditions, excess fluid in the body.

Venus in Capricorn
Arthritis in the knees, swollen knees, rheumatic pains in thighs, gout.

Venus in Aquarius
Congestive heart failure, poor venous circulation, varicose veins, swelling in the legs, dropsy, swollen knees.

Venus in Pisces
Lameness in the feet, swellings in the legs, catarrhal conditions, diarrhoea, flatulence.

MERCURY

Mercury is dignified in Gemini and Virgo, the signs of its rulership. It is in detriment in Sagittarius and Pisces. Mercury is also said to be exalted in Virgo and have its fall in Pisces. The nature of Mercury accords with the Ether Element, the vital force that flows through the body.

Mercury, like the Moon, is also connected with the brain and nervous system. Mercury can be visualised as representing the flow of energy through the nervous system. Since Mercury embraces mental

experience, especially the rational mind, it particularly represents that part of the nervous system under our conscious control. Mercury rules the tongue, by extension it also rules the voice. Languages are also linked to Mercury, the word language comes from the Latin *lingua* meaning 'a tongue'. Essentially through the tongue ideas are expressed as the spoken word.

Mercury also rules the arms, hands, legs and feet. In other words Mercury rules the limbs which, through the motor nervous system, enables ideas to be translated into actions. Mercury also rules the skin, so Mercury is also very strongly involved with the sense of touch.

Mercurial diseases

In general the Mercurial characteristics of disease, since Ether embodies all the primary qualities of the Elements, can be hot, cold, dry and moist.

The diseases of Mercury can be divided to two main categories:

- neurological disorders where disease affects the brain and nervous system disturbing its normal function
- where disease is perceived to be of a mental origin disrupting the nervous state of the person.

Of the neurological disorders, Mercury rules such conditions as vertigo, convulsions and paralysis.

Of the mental disturbances linked to Mercury these include madness, vain imaginations, disturbed intellect, anxiety, negative thought patterns, sensual distraction, delirium.

Table 6.7 Diseases associated with Mercury in particular signs

Mercury in Aries
Neurological disease, vertigo, facial spasms, cranial neuralgia, insomnia, sexual difficulties, impotence.

Mercury in Taurus
Inflammation in the throat, lymphadenitis or swollen lymph nodes on the neck, laryngitis, aphonia, hoarseness, pains in the feet.

Mercury in Gemini
Bilious flatulence, gout in the hand, pains in the arms, nervous eczema.

Mercury in Cancer
Asthma, cold stomach, gastro-intestinal spasms and griping, mucus in stomach, loss of appetite, lameness, nervous debility.

Mercury in Leo
Nervous trembling, shock, cardiac arhythmias, pains in the back, depression.

Mercury in Virgo
Flatulent dyspepsia, colic, intestinal spasm, neurological pain, shortness of breath.

Mercury in Libra
Kidney infection, dysuria, strangury, obstructions, haematological disorders, asthma, eczema.

Mercury in Scorpio
Inflammations of sexual organs, endometriosis, sexual difficulties, incontinence, rectal spasm, rheumatic pains in arms and shoulders.

Mercury in Sagittarius
Kidney disease, weakness in the back, anorexia nervosa, nervous cough, swellings in the hips and thighs.

Mercury in Capricorn
Dysuria, gout, arthritis in knees, pains in the back, depression.

Mercury in Aquarius
Anxiety, nervousness, neuralgia, fleeting pains throughout body, nervous eczema, diarrhoea, intestinal disorders, cholera.

Mercury in Pisces
Head pain, poor motor control in the legs and feet, gonorrhoea, kidney infections.

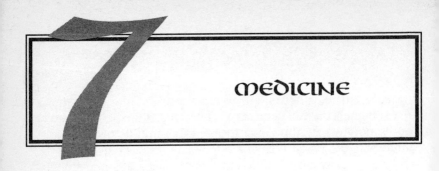

MEDICINE

Herbs and plants exert an extraordinary fascination for people. Who has not witnessed the marvel of looking each morning and seeing how much plants have grown during the night? When climatic conditions or, as we have seen, when the Elements are in balance growth is very rapid. It was the observation of such marvels that led the ancient herbalists to consider each plant as possessing its own vital force.

The plant's vital force was called its virtue and seen to confer the healing properties and medicinal actions on the body. Immense importance has been placed upon correctly understanding the virtues of plants from direct observation. To understand the virtues of plants herbalists have been trained to look at their physical form, taste, smell and where they like to grow.

One of the techniques used is to project the five Elements on to the plant kingdom so that the Earth Element corresponds to the roots, the Water Element corresponds to the stem or trunk, the Air Element corresponds to the leaves and the Fire Element corresponds to the flowers. Ether corresponds to the vital force or virtue contained in the sap. By the time a plant flowers it has evolved through four stages of Elemental development – from root to stem, to leaf, to flower – so that in turn Ether, the quintessence, is transmuted into the seeds. On germination a seed releases the vital force encapsulated within it generating the four Elements that compose the new plant.

By looking at the most developed part of a plant it is possible to see which Element it has the greatest affinity with. For example, clivers (*Galium aparine* – see Figure 7.1) has long trailing stems that rambles through the English hedgerows in the summer months. Its roots are tiny, its leaves are small and its white flowers are tiny. Since the stem is the most developed part of the plant, so the herb has greatest affinity with the Water Element. In turn, the herb has an affinity with the Water Element in the body. This is reflected in the medicinal uses of clivers, which include reducing inflammation in the lymphatic system and enhancing circulation of lymph around the body. The herb is also a useful diuretic which removes fluid via the kidneys and helps eliminate toxins from the body.

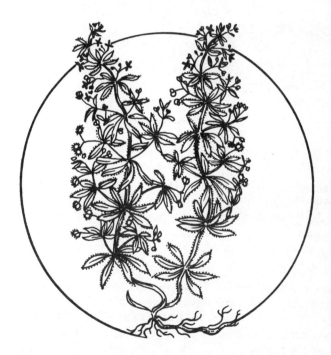

Figure 7.1 Clivers (*Galium aparine*) from Gerard, *The Herbal*, 1633

Figure 7.2 Willow (*Salix alba*) from Gerard, *The Herbal*, 1633

However, the most important technique used to understand a herb's virtues is to designate a planetary ruler. Once the planetary ruler is identified the medicinal uses are then worked out using symbolic correspondences. The willow (*Salix alba* – see Figure 7.2) the tree famous for being one of the sources of the drug Aspirin provides a clear example.

The willow has been associated with the Moon since the time of classical Greece. Like the Moon, the Lunar virtue of willow can be seen by the tree's affinity for water. It typically likes to grow next to streams, rivers and lakes. Its leaves also have a characteristic silvery lustre, again like the Moon. It is no coincidence that a willow frond is traditionally chosen as the preferred medium by dowsers seeking to find water underground.

Once the Lunar rulership is made, the herb can be seen to have an affinity with the parts of the body ruled by the Moon. As already seen in Chapter 6, these included the lungs, stomach, bladder and breasts. In particular, the willow was used for treating lung infections.

Willow has an ancient reputation for allaying fever, its Watery virtue putting out the excess Fire in the body. The Moon with its affinity for the lungs makes the willow particularly appropriate for dealing with chest infections associated with fever.

The validity of these ancient ideas is confirmed by modern pharmacology. The main active constituent is salicylic acid which is commonly known, in a slightly different, form as the drug Aspirin. Amongst a range of pharmacological actions, salicylic acid powerfully reduces the body temperature by increasing sweating.

The virtues of herbs are also classified by temperatures, that is whether they are hot, cold, wet or dry. This classification of temperature which was first made by the Roman physician Galen. It is predominantly based upon taste. The sensation of a particular herb on the tongue, enables the herbalist to visualise the effect the herb has on the vital force in the body generally. For example, cucumber has a cold and moist taste which demonstrates that it has a cooling and moistening action on the vital force. By contrast, ginger has a hot and dry taste which demonstrates that it has a heating and drying action on the vital force.

Where the herb has an affinity with a particular organ of the body, as in the case of the willow and the lungs, the action on the vital force is then specifically directed to that part of the body. Willow has a cold and dry taste revealing it has a cooling and drying action on the vital force. The effect of the herb upon the lungs is that it cools the inflammation and dries up the secretion of phlegm. An action that made the herb extremely useful in the treatment of chest infections.

This combination of understanding the virtue of a herb through a planetary ruler and knowing its action on the vital force from the temperature, enabled herbalists to derive very precise insights into the uses of herbs.

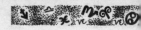

Furthermore, some herbs in addition to a planetary ruler are also associated with a zodiacal sign. The zodiacal sign reflects the places where they grow. The principle here is that the virtue of a herb also absorbs the energy of the place wherein it grows. Though there are plants, like the dandelion (*Taraxacum officinale*) and nettle (*Urtica dioica*), that grow across a wide range of terrains there are certain herbs, like the sundew (*Droscera rotundifolia* – see Figure 7.3), that are only able to grow in one particular habitat. These are the herbs that have a zodiacal sign in addition to the planetary ruler. The sundew is ruled by the Sun in Cancer, for it is found growing only amongst spagnum moss beds in acid marshlands.

Figure 7.3 Sundew (*Droscera rotundifolia*) from Gerard, *The Herbal*, 1633

Places associated with each of the zodiacal signs are partly based upon the Elemental ruler of the sign. Simply, Fire signs are associated with fiery places such as kilns and forges. Water signs are associated with wet places such as ditches, lakes and marshes. Air signs are associated with windy places such as exposed hills or clearings in woods. Earth signs are associated with earthly places such as meadows and mines. The Water sign of Cancer is specifically linked with boggy marshland, hence the Cancerian connection to the sundew.

The solar rulership of sundew comes from the round green leaves which turn bright red the more the sun shines on them. The hotter the sun the more intense the red colour becomes. The leaves are covered by tiny red hairs which secrete sugary juices at their tips to attract insects.

The secretions too are most abundant when the sun is hottest, from which the plant gets the name sundew. The attracted insects get stuck to the hairs and, as they struggle to get free, more hairs curl over further trapping them. The leaves then secrete digestive enzymes to dissolve the nutriment from the insects. This clasping property of the plant can also be seen as being Cancerian.

The additional zodiacal sign leads to very specific uses of the herb. Just as the herb only grows in a specific zodiacal environment, so the planetary virtue of the herb is particularly directed to those parts of the body ruled by the same zodiacal sign. In the case of the sundew the Cancerian rulership specifically directs the solar virtue of the herb to the chest and lungs – ruled by Cancer – where its hot and dry action dries up the secretions of phlegm. Specifically, sundew is used for treating asthma and chronic bronchitis. It contains plumbagin, an antibiotic substance that kills a wide range of bacteria that infect the respiratory system.

Astrology has also been used to gather herbs at the time of their optimum virtue. Culpeper gives an example in his description of greater celandine (*Chelidonium majus* – see Figure 7.4):

This is an herb of the Sun, and under the Celestial Lion, and is one of the best cures for the eyes, for all that know anything in astrology know that the eyes are subject to the Luminaries: let it be gathered when the Sun is in Leo, and the Moon in Aries, applying to this time: let Leo arise, then may you make it into an oil or ointment, which you please, to anoint your sore eyes with:

Figure 7.4 Greater Celandine (*Chelidonium majus*) from Gerard, *The Herbal*, 1633

Celandine is a solar herb, so the time of its optimum virtue is when the Sun is dignified in Leo – the sign the Sun rules. Furthermore, he describes in the preparation of the eye ointment that the Moon needs to be in Aries. In this sign the Moon directs the virtue of the herbs to the head, enhancing the healing of the eyes. This lunar principle can be used to direct the healing influence of the medicine to any particular part of the body that is diseased.

8

medical
astrology
in action

In the previous chapters various aspects of astrological symbolism, in relation to health and disease, have been explained. This chapter will demonstrate how this knowledge is applied to an astrological chart. In marked contrast to the prevailing conception of astrology as solely being based upon the time of a person's birth – the, so called, natal astrology – the astrology of health is traditionally based upon the physical event of a person becoming ill. The time is taken from when a patient falls ill or decides to go to bed. The name for this branch of astrology is decumbiture, which comes from the Latin word decumbo meaning 'to lie down or to fall'. It was through using such times that herbal physicians, such as Nicholas Culpeper, made their judgements of diagnosis, prognosis and choice of herbs.

Space in this book does not permit a demonstration of how you draw up an astrological chart or provide a thorough explanation of decumbiture. Please see the Further Reading list to take the subject further. This chapter will simply describe the bare bones of the technique, so that readers can see how all the aspects covered in the book are drawn together and illustrated in a case history. The therapeutic principles of decumbiture has been intentionally omitted.

The moment of illness

There are a number of possible moments on which to base a decumbiture. Firstly, the moment when the patient feels so overcome by their illness that they have got to lie down. This is the

truest time to judge a decumbiture, however not everyone takes to their bed when unwell, even if they would like to. Alternatively, if a disease starts suddenly following an accident or some other specific event, this time can also be used. Frequently, patients have totally forgotten when they first felt unwell, in which case the time of first visiting the medical practitioner, therapist or counsellor can be used instead. This is essentially the time when a patient is prompted by their illness to seek help and advice. This is by far the most available time for basing the decumbiture, particularly when many have difficulty recalling the year in which they first felt unwell let alone the day and time when their illness started. A phone call often means that the time of first contact between a practitioner and patient is quite separate from the time of the first consultation. When known, the time of the telephone conversation is to be preferred over the time of the first consultation, since this is when the patient is prompted into doing something about their state of health, as opposed to when the practitioner is available for consultation.

However, in the absence of a preliminary conversation the time of the first appointment can be used with impressive results. Early or late arrivals for their appointments can also be significant in this respect. Another useful time may be when blood or urine tests are done in order to find out what is happening in the body.

Understanding a Decumbiture Chart

The decumbiture chart is an event chart of a person becoming ill, consequently its interpretation is distinctly different from reading a natal chart. The interpretation of decumbiture specifically focuses on five of the twelve houses, as can be seen in Figure 8.1. These houses are:

1 The first house which describes the patient's body, their health and vitality.
2 The sixth house which describes the patient's disease.
3 The seventh house which describes the judgement of physician/astrologer.

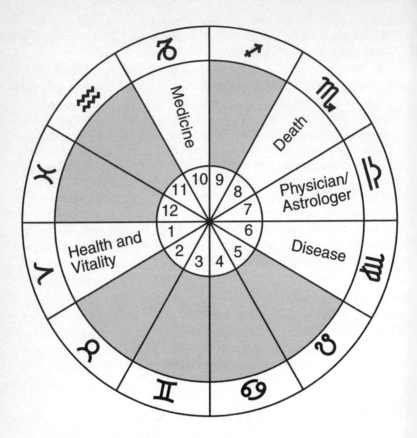

Figure 8.1 The houses used in decumbiture

4 The eighth house which reflects the patient's death.
5 The tenth house which describes the medicines needed to help the patient.

The symbolic link between these houses and the patient with their illness is made through the zodiac signs that are found on the house cusps, together with the corresponding planetary rulers. This process is called ascribing signification. For example, if the sign of Taurus is found at the ascendant (the first house cusp) then Venus, which rules Taurus, specifically signifies the patient and their health and

vitality in the decumbiture chart. Venus is consequently described as the significator of the patient. The same technique is repeated for the sixth, seventh, eighth and tenth houses, to find the significators for the patient's illness, therapist, death and medicine respectively.

Just as the Moon moves the waters of the oceans so, symbolically, the Moon is seen to influence the flow of vital force through the body. For this reason in decumbiture the Moon is seen as an additional significator of the patient's disease, for she reflects the course and unfoldment of the illness.

To demonstrate the astrology of decumbiture in action, please see the 'Bee sting chart' in Figure 8.2, a simple incident of a bee sting created at a precise moment on which to base a decumbiture.

> *I had been studying medical astrology for most of a morning when I decided that it must be lunchtime. However, when I saw the kitchen clock, I realised that it was too early for lunch. I decided instead to return to my studies. Precisely at that moment the kitchen door burst open and in rushed one of our herbal dispensers. 'Dylan, Dylan I have just been stung, what shall I put on the sting?' She dramatically exclaimed.*

> *She had been outside gathering lime flower blossoms to make into a tincture, when she was stung by a bee on her right hand, at the tip of the index finger. Closer inspection revealed the sting embedded in her finger with the venom sacs still pulsating and injecting the venom into it. I immediately pulled the sting out with my finger nails and then rushed to get an onion. I quickly cut the onion in two and pushed her finger tip into one of the halves.*

> *Onion is an effective remedy for bee and wasp stings when it is applied immediately after the incident. After two minutes all pain and swelling had gone from her finger tip. When I resumed my studies I suddenly realised I had noted the time just before the door burst open. This proved to be particularly fascinating.*

For the purpose of illustration, for those who are unfamiliar with astrological concepts, the sequence of signification in this chart has been simplified by using letters of the alphabet. Please look for the letters in sequence in Figure 8.2. The ascendant (A) is 9°50' Libra.

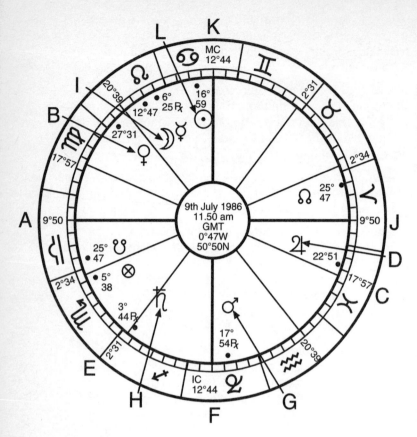

Figure 8.2 The bee sting chart

As Venus (B) rules Libra, her placing at 27°31' Leo in the 11th house indicates the dispenser. The 6th house cusp (C) is 17°57' Pisces. As Jupiter (D) rules Pisces, he signifies the dispenser's disease. Appropriately Jupiter is located in his own sign at 22°51' Pisces, in the 6th house of illness. Additionally, the 6th house also traditionally rules work, while its ruler Jupiter, according to Nicholas Culpeper, rules lime trees (*Tilea europea* – Figure 8.3). Furthermore the 6th house also rules small animals, so Jupiter is the significator

Figure 8.3 Lime tree (*Tilea europea*) from Gerard, *The Herbal*, 1633

for the bee. This signification is particularly appropriate since bees are also traditionally ruled by Jupiter. Jupiter is mythologically King of the Gods who acts out his authority by throwing down thunder bolts from the heavens. Bees have long been noted by bee keepers to be particularly sensitive to thunder storms. At the first flash of lightning they immediately fly back to their hive, hence they are seen to be under the rulership of Jupiter. This combination of symbolism reflects that the dispenser, in her work, was harvesting lime flowers when she was stung by the bee that caused her disease.

Anatomically the sequence of the twelve houses reflects the parts of the body connected with zodiacal signs. So that the first house through its association with Aries is also connected with the head. The second house is connected with the neck and shoulders and so on through the sequence, finishing with twelfth house and the feet.

Since the 3rd house cusp (E), linked to the arms and hands, is found at 2°31' Sagittarius, Jupiter (D) also rules the dispenser's hands. This combination of symbolism precisely links the disease with her hand. Furthermore, Jupiter's location in the Western hemisphere (placed to the right of the 4th/10th axis (F/K) – at 12°44' Capricorn/Cancer) of the chart specifically indicates that her left hand is diseased.

Stings are naturally ruled by Mars, the fiery god of war. Mars (G) is located at 17°54' Capricorn separating from a sextile (60°) aspect to Jupiter at 22°50' of Pisces. Its retrograde or backward motion accentuating the separation between the Planets. This separating aspect suggests the bee going off to die leaving its sting in the dispenser's index finger.

A detail further reflected by Saturn (H) at 3°44' Sagittarius also retrograde in motion and placed (conjunct) at the 3rd house cusp. The arrows of Sagittarius the archer additionally suggest stings and burning. Saturn retrograding on to the third house cusp also reflects the sting firmly embedded into her finger. Jupiter's hot and moist nature located in the Water sign Pisces is particularly descriptive of the inflammation and swelling associated with stings.

The Moon (I) cosignificator of the disease, located at 12°47' Leo – a Fire sign, indicates the burning pain she must have felt with the sting. As Leo is also associated with theatre, this placing of the Moon is also descriptive of the dispenser's dramatic entrance through the door.

The 7th house cusp (J) which rules the physician is 9°50' Aries, since Mars (G) rules Aries I am thereby shown by Mars. Despite its retrograde motion, Mars is strongly placed in Capricorn the sign of its exaltation, indicating I was in a good position to cure the patient.

The 10th house cusp (K) shows the medicine. As the 10th house cusp is located at 12°44' Cancer, the Moon rules the medicine. The selection of the onion as a remedy was entirely appropriate as onions are traditionally under the dominion of both Mars and the Moon. Since the Moon is in the Fire sign of Leo, the hot and dry temperature of the onion can be seen to counter the swelling indicated by Jupiter in Pisces (cold and moist).

There is a powerful mutual reception (a relationship between two Planets occupying positions of each other's rulership, whereby they can symbolically swap places) between the Sun and Moon. The Sun (L) is placed at 16°59' Cancer, the sign ruled by the Moon. Correspondingly, the Moon (I) is placed at 12°47' Leo, the sign ruled by the Sun. Both of the luminaries are located in the 10th house of medicine and healing. Since the Sun generates the vital force and the Moon circulates it around the body, this is a particularly potent indication of the dispenser's speedy recovery.

The most compelling detail of this decumbiture chart once more returns to Jupiter ruling the dispenser's hands (3rd house cusp) and her disease (6th house cusp). The index finger on which she was stung is traditionally associated in cheiromancy with the energies of Jupiter, hence the name Jupiter finger!

exploring medical astrology

In order to understand more about medical astrology it is best to study real case histories. I would strongly recommend that you calculate and draw up charts/obtain computer printouts for times when illness started or accidents happened. However it is not recommended that you study a current illness as there is a risk of becoming too emotionally involved in the chart. Alternatively, have any of your friends or family members had any significant illness or accidents that you could use? Can you find times and dates for these events? Old diaries are a useful source, or a medical practioner or therapist might be able to tell you the time and date of the first consultation with them. If you are not medically qualified yourself, can you obtain the collaboration of a doctor or other therapist sympathetic to your interest? Such a relationship may considerably help your studies by providing illness/ consultation times as well as medical details.

For a personal event take some time to write down your experience of the illness. Describe how you felt, note down the

various symptoms, in sequence if possible, and where they occurred in the body, note how long the illness and/or the symptoms lasted, note anything that made it better or worse.

Similarly, for a friend or family member, ask them the above points and note them down. As you take the case history particularly note how they describe the illness. Are they reserved or reluctant to describe their medical history? This is typical of the Earth Element. Are they overly dramatic in the telling of their story? This is typical of the Fire Element. Are they deeply emotional in describing their symptoms, possibly moved to tears? This is typical of the Water Element. Are they detached and aloof in sharing their personal story with you and possibly vague in the memory of details? This is typical of the Air Element.

EVALUATING THE CHART

OBSERVATIONS ON THE PATIENT'S HEALTH

In each decumbiture chart, look at the Ascendant and the planet which rules it and see how the symbols describe the patient, their health and vitality. Consider the zodiacal sign at the Ascendant; does it concord in any way to the patient's own natal Sun or Ascendant sign? A typical Sun sign description found in such books as Graham Boston's *Astrology – a beginner's guide*, may well help your understanding of the physical appearance and personality of the patient. Note which Element is linked to the zodiacal sign and see how this describes their vitality.

Fire signs have a strong vitality, quickly recover from illness though are prone to stress. Earth signs have a sluggish metabolism, however are generally robust in health. Water signs have a weak vitality and are vulnerable to illness, especially of an emotional cause. Air signs though vulnerable to illness have a stronger vitality than Water, however they are prone to mental or nervous disorders.

Whatever planet rules the Ascendant, it specifically describes the patient's vitality, so the condition in which it is found has a direct bearing on what is happening to their vitality at that moment in

the chart. Is the ruler of the Ascendant located in the sign of its rulership or exaltation? For example, if Aries is the sign at the Ascendant, than Mars is the planetary ruler of the Ascendant. If Mars is located in either Aries or Scorpio where it is dignified or in Capricorn where it is exalted, then it shows that the patient's vitality is particularly strong.

Alternatively, is the ruler of the Ascendant located in the opposite sign to its rulership or exaltation? For example, if Mars is located in either Libra or Taurus where it is in detriment or in Cancer where it has its fall, then it shows that the patient's vitality is especially weak.

Note, too, how the nature of the planet, whether it is hot, cold, moist or dry, interacts with the Elemental nature of the sign in which it is located. For example, if Mars is located in Leo, the hot and dry nature of Mars concords with the hot and dry nature of the Fire sign, indicating an intensification of their vitality. Conversely, if Mars is located in Pisces, the hot and dry nature of Mars is extinguished by the cold and moist nature of the Water sign, indicating a weakening of their vitality.

Does the ruler of the Ascendant have any aspects of either Saturn or Mars? The aspects include the conjunction (0 °), opposition (180 °), square (90 °), trine (120 °) and sextile (60 °) – see Graham Boston's *Astrology – a beginner's guide*, for a more detailed explanation of aspects. Saturn and Mars by both positive and negative aspects weaken the ruler of the Ascendant, in turn indicating the weakening of the patient's vitality.

Does the ruler of the Ascendant have any aspects to either Jupiter or Venus? Jupiter and Venus by both positive and negative aspects strengthen the ruler of the Ascendant, in turn indicating the strengthening of the patient's vitality. If the ruler of the Ascendant is retrograde this indicates a weakening of the patient's vitality.

In all decumbiture charts assess the condition of the Sun as this planet represents the generation of the patient's vitality. Consider the same points as noted for the ruler of the Ascendant. If the

Sun is in a weak state then the patient's supply of vital energy is poor. Conversely, if the Sun is in a strong position then the patient's supply of vital energy is sound.

Similarly, assess the condition of the Moon as this planet relates to the circulation of the patient's vitality around the body. If the Moon is in a weak state then the circulation of the patient's vital energy is poor. Conversely, if the Moon is in a strong position then the circulation of the patient's vital energy is vigorous. Also, in noting in what sign the Moon is located, this strongly reflects how the patient felt in the course of their illness; compare this to how they told their story.

IDENTIFICATION OF THE PATIENT'S DISEASE

Next in the decumbiture chart, look at the 6th house cusp and the planet which rules it and see how the symbols describe the patient's disease. Consult the appropriate table in Chapter 6 to see how the symbolism fits in with the diagnosis of the disease in the case history. If the tables does not hold true, the location of the illness may also be shown by the sign at the 6th house cusp, or by the sign the ruler of the 6th house is placed in, or by the planetary ruler itself. Note which Elements are linked to the zodiacal signs involved and see how they describe the symptoms of the disease.

Fire signs are associated with hot and dry symptoms such as fever, inflammation and burning pain. Earth signs are associated with cold and dry symptoms such as stagnation, blockages, dull and persistent aches. Water signs are associated with cold and moist symptoms such as swellings, discharges, chills, shivering and spasmodic pain. Air signs are associated with hot and moist symptoms such as wind, hyperventilation and radiating pain.

Whatever planet rules the 6th house, it specifically indicates patient's disease, so the condition in which it is found has a direct bearing on how the disease is affecting them. Is the ruler of the 6th house located in the sign of its rulership or exaltation? In

which case the disease is strong. Alternatively, is the ruler of the 6th house located in the opposite sign to its rulership or exaltation? In which case the disease is weak. Again note how the nature of the planet interacts with the Elemental nature of the sign it is located in. How does that strengthen or weaken the disease?

Does the ruler of the 6th house have any aspects to either Saturn or Mars? Both Saturn and Mars by both positive and negative aspects to the ruler of the 6th house strengthen the nature of the disease. Saturn indicates a chronic disease while Mars indicates an acute disease.

Does the ruler of the 6th house have any aspects to either Jupiter or Venus? Jupiter or Venus by both positive and negative aspects to the ruler of the 6th house weaken the nature of the disease, as both planets enhance the flow of vital force in the body.

Also, note whether the sign on the 6th house cusp or the sign the ruler of the 6th house is cardinal, fixed or mutable. Cardinal signs are descriptive of a disease that either quickly resolves or rapidly worsens. Fixed signs are descriptive of a disease that is firmly entrenched in the body and hard to resolve. Mutable signs are descriptive of a disease that waxes and wanes in its intensity or has a recurrent nature. If the ruler of the 6th house is retrograde this also indicates the chronic nature of the disease.

assessment of health

Having made all the above observations on the patient's health and vitality and identified the nature of their disease in the chart, it is now possible to make an assessment of their overall health. Which is the strongest planet between the ruler of the Ascendant and ruler of the 6th house in the chart?

If the ruler of the Ascendant is stronger than the ruler of the 6th house, then the patient's vitality is stronger than the disease and so they will be able to overcome it and get better. Conversely if

the ruler of the Ascendant is weaker than the ruler of the 6th house, then the patient's vitality is weaker than the disease and so they will be unable to overcome it, unless therapeutically the patient's vitality is enhanced with diet, herbs and exercise while the nature of the disease is weakened.

Note, too, any aspects between the rulers of the Ascendant and the 6th house. A conjunction, opposition or a square would indicate a struggle of the patient's vitality in overcoming the disease, whereas a trine or sextile would indicate the disease is easily resolved.

In conclusion, I hope that you have found this introduction to medical astrology valuable and through doing some medical charts for yourself you have been inspired to take the study further. The Further Reading section contains titles which more comprehensively explore the subject, while the Useful Addresses contains contacts for organisations should you wish to take the subject more seriously.

fURTheR READING

Boston, Graham, *Astrology – a beginner's guide*, Hodder & Stoughton, 1998

Culpeper, Nicholas, *Culpeper's Complete Herbal*, Foulsham – a contemporary format of his 1654 herbal.

Culpeper, Nicholas, *Astrological Judgement of Diseases*, 1655, reprinted Ascella Publications, 1993

Lilly, William, *Christian Astrology*, 1647, reprinted Regulus, 1985

Thulesius, Olav, *Nicholas Culpeper*, St Martin's Press, 1992

Tobyn, Graeme, *Culpeper's Medicine*, Element, 1997

Warren-Davis, Dylan, *The Hand Reveals*, Element, 1993

Warren-Davis, Dylan, *An Introduction to Decumbiture*, article series within *The Traditional Astrologer* magazine, Ascella Publications, Issues 1–16

useful addresses

Astrological Organisations

The Astrological Association, 396 Caledonian Road, London,
  N1 1DN, UK. Tel: 0171 700 3746; Fax: 0171 700 6479.
The Company of Astrologers,
  PO Box 3001, London, N1 1LY, UK. Tel: 01227 362427.
Federation of Australian Astrologers Inc., 24 Berryman Street, North
  Ryde, New South Wales 2113, Australia. e mail: faa@peg.apc.org.
Canadian Association for Astrological Education, 4191 Stonemason
  Crescent, Mississauga, Ontario L51 2Z6, Canada.
Astrological Society of South Africa, PO Box 2968, Rivonia 2128,
  Gauteng, South Africa. Tel: (+27)-11-867-4153.
American Federation of Astrologers, PO Box 22040, 6535 South
  Rural Road, Tempe, Arizona 85285-2040, USA. Tel: 602-838-1751;
  Fax: 602-838-8293.

Herbal Organisations

National Institute of Medical Herbalists, 56 Longbrook Street,
  Exeter, Devon EX4 6AH, UK. Tel: 01392 426022
National Herbalists Association of Australia, Suite 14, 247–249
  Kingsgrove Road, (PO Box 65), Kingsgrove, New South Wales
  2208, Australia.
American Botanical Council, PO Box 201660, Austin, Texas 78720-
  1040, USA.

Dylan Warren-Davis
Tuition, Lectures, Readings and Consultations, 13 Myrtle Street,
Murwillumbah, New South Wales 2484, Australia.
Tel: (+612) /02 6672 8427

A BEGINNER'S GUIDE

ASTROLOGY

Graham Boston

Since the dawn of civilization people have measured time against the movements of the heavenly bodies, while seeing in the stars a reflection of life on earth. From its origins in predicting the outcome of battles and the success or failure of annual crops, astrology has evolved into a rich and subtle language that gives a new perspective to all areas of human experience.

In the beginner's guide, Graham Boston explores how astrology enables us to understand ourselves, other people and our relationships more fully. In a series of simple, practical steps he also describes how to draw up and interpret a horoscope, the map of the heavens that is the basis of the astrologer's art.

'Every so often, a series of books comes along which stands out against the run-of-the-mill publications. This is such a collection. These books should be on everyone's shelves. Do yourself a favour and get the whole set.'

A BEGINNER'S GUIDE

NUMEROLOGY

Kristyna Arcarti

Numerology is fun, easy and scientifically based, yet requires no psychic skills or great mathematical talents to understand. *Numerology – a beginner's guide* is a concise but comprehensive introduction to the ancient art of numerology. It gives you all the information you require to understand the significance of numbers and how they can affect your life.

The book explains the different numerological systems, giving detailed meanings, examples and exercises to help you to understand the following:

- life numbers
- name numbers
- expression numbers
- heart numbers
- destiny numbers
- fadic numbers

Numerology – a beginner's guide also looks at ways you can use this science to gauge compatibility between people – useful both on a business and a personal level.

NUMEROLOGY AND RELATIONSHIPS

John C. Burford

Numerology and Relationships takes you step by step through the hidden meanings behind the important numbers in your life. It explains how an understanding of numerology can reveal the major issues and energies of your Life Path and Life Purpose. In this easy-to-follow guide you will learn how to: analyse your relationships using numerology; discover your compatibilities with others – especially your partner; understand the crucial relationships with your parents; be prepared for the major issues affecting each period of your children's lives.

John C. Burford has had a lifelong fascination for numbers. He was born with a Life Path of 5 (lots of travel and many careers) and a Life Purpose of 21/3 (he likes people and is a spiritual healer).

'Every so often, a series of books comes along which stands out against the run-of-the-mill publications. This is such a collection. These books should be on everyone's shelves. Do yourself a favour and get the whole set.'